七绝古诗英译选

Selected Translatings of Chinese Seven-character Quatrains

杜洪峰　译著

黑龙江人民出版社

图书在版编目（CIP）数据

七绝古诗英译选／杜洪峰译著. — 哈尔滨：黑龙
江人民出版社，2016.7（2020.8重印）
ISBN 978-7-207-10782-4

Ⅰ.①七… Ⅱ.①杜… Ⅲ.①古典诗歌—诗集—中国
—英文 Ⅳ.①I222.7

中国版本图书馆CIP数据核字（2016）第181844号

责任编辑：王　琳　李文越
封面设计：张　涛

七绝古诗英译选

杜洪峰　译著

出版发行　黑龙江人民出版社
地　　址　哈尔滨市南岗区宣庆小区1号楼
邮　　编　150008
网　　址　www.longpress.com
电子邮箱　hljrmcbs@yeah.net
印　　刷　山东华立印务有限公司
开　　本　787×1092　1/16
印　　张　13.5
字　　数　200千字
版　　次　2016年8月第1版　2020年8月第3次印刷
书　　号　ISBN 978-7-207-10782-4
定　　价　27.00元

版权所有　侵权必究　　　举报电话：（0451）82308054
法律顾问：北京市大成律师事务所哈尔滨分所律师赵学利、赵景波

目　录 / Contents

目 录

目录

4

目 录

Contents

目 录

目 录

12

目 录

渡 湘 江

唐　杜审言

迟日园林悲昔游，

今春花鸟作边愁。

独怜京国人南窜，

不似湘江水北流。

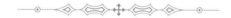

Across the Xiang River

Sighing over the good old days when I went spring outing, relishing the beauty of many a garden,

Despite the blooming flowers and singing birds, I had to keep forging to the frontier as an exile, sorrow–laden.

What a shame that people fled flooding from the Capital to the south, panic–stricken,

On the contrary, the Xiang River kept bearing north through the war–trodden.

回乡偶书

唐　贺知章

少小离家老大回，

乡音无改鬓毛衰。

儿童相见不相识，

笑问客从何处来。

My Spent Youth,
a Poem Improvised on My Way Home

I left my hometown a juvenile and returned an old man,

With hair turning grey and thin, still I spoke as then.

Face to face, I looked a stranger to a boy of my clan,

"Where do you come from?" Smiled and asked the son.

咏 柳

唐 贺知章

碧玉妆成一树高，

万条垂下绿丝绦。

不知细叶谁裁出，

二月春风似剪刀。

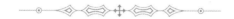

Willows

As lushly green as jasper, the willow stands a graceful young lady,

With drooping branches very much the image of green ribbons swaying gently.

How come its leaves so slim and curvy?

As if magically, they're trimmed so by a pair of invisible scissors, the spring breeze prevailing in February.

凉 州 词

唐　王翰

葡萄美酒夜光杯，

欲饮琵琶马上催。

醉卧沙场君莫笑，

古来征战几人回？

An Episode Before the War

Jade cups brimmed with wine were lustrous at night,

Between alcohol and melody, for combating the warriors were
inflamed an appetite.

Lying drunk on the battlefield was not quite a sight,

After all, few of them were likely to survive the coming bloody
fight.

凉 州 词

唐　王之涣

黄河远上白云间，

一片孤城万仞山。

羌笛何须怨杨柳，

春风不度玉门关。

Between Battles

The Yellow River seems rushing down from the sky, an expanse of
whiteness,

Mountains of dizzy height are besieging a frontier fortress standing
in loneliness.

Blameless is the *Zheyangliu*, a nomadic flute tune, dripping with
sadness,

For the Yumen Pass is perennially beyond the reach of vernal
breezes, a herald of liveliness.

芙蓉楼送辛渐

唐　王昌龄

寒雨连江夜入吴，

平明送客楚山孤。

洛阳亲友如相问，

一片冰心在玉壶。

Seeing off Xin Jian, My Friend,
at Furong Tower

Last night, a cold rain was prevailing over the rivers and lands of
southeastern China,

The distant mountains a looming presence, the sorrow of parting
came over my friend and me bidding farewell to each other.

If you were to meet at Luoyang my acquaintances, and by them I
were inquired after,

Do tell them I would remain as steadfast and faithful as ever.

出　塞·其一
唐　王昌龄

秦时明月汉时关，

万里长征人未还。

但使龙城飞将在，

不教胡马度阴山。

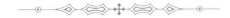

The First *Beyond the Warring Frontier*

Back to the Qin and Han Dynasties, a cold moon overlooked a
frontier fortress confronting an ancient battleground,
Embarking on a crusade against the enemy, most soldiers had
perished in action, their bones nowhere to be found.
Should General Huo Qubing and his invincible army still patrol
around,
Nomadic invaders would suffer a hard blow, their horses fall and
their chariots rebound.

出　塞·其二

唐　王昌龄

骝马新跨白玉鞍，

战罢沙场月色寒。

城头铁鼓声犹振，

匣里金刀血未干。

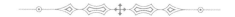

The Second *Beyond the Warring Frontier*

Astride a black steed with a white saddle, a general charged fearlessly,

After the battle, the field was deadly still under a moon staring emotionlessly.

From above a gate tower came bursts of drumbeat rumbling thunderously,

Sheathing their sabers stained by fresh blood, warriors stood undefeated, staring into the distance triumphantly.

从军行七首·其四

唐　王昌龄

青海长云暗雪山，

孤城遥望玉门关。

黄沙百战穿金甲，

不破楼兰终不还。

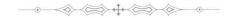

The Fourth *Between Battles*

Dark clouds were looming up above Qinghai Lake, and around it

the snow−mantled mountains took on a look dim and formidable,

A long way from the Yumen Pass was another frontier fortress

standing alone and impregnable.

Soldiers' armor had been worn through between fierce sandstorms

and battles innumerable,

Their resolution to crush the enemy remained persistent and

unshakable.

闺 怨

唐 王昌龄

闺中少妇不知愁，

春日凝妆上翠楼。

忽见陌头杨柳色，

悔教夫婿觅封侯。

A Rueful Young Wife

A young wife might otherwise lead a sweet life free from anything bitter,

A fine spring day, she spruced herself up and went upstairs in her best bib and tucker.

Suddenly, a fit of grief came over her at the sight of street-side willows making a lively picture.

What a remorse that she had sent her husband to the army for rank and honor!

渭城曲／送元二使安西

唐　王维

渭城朝雨浥轻尘，

客舍青青柳色新。

劝君更尽一杯酒，

西出阳关无故人。

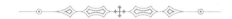

Seeing off a Friend at the Wei City

A morning drizzle had settled the rising dust in the city,

Nestling behind green willows was an inn painted freshly.

I proposed one more toast to my friend about to take a long journey,

Forging further west until Yangguan, a remote frontier fortress, was left behind, you would have anything but a friend's company.

九月九日忆山东兄弟

唐　王维

独在异乡为异客，

每逢佳节倍思亲。

遥知兄弟登高处，

遍插茱萸少一人。

A Recall of My Siblings on Chung Yeung Festival

An expatriate adrift on a strange land,

I feel my heart burning with homesickness when the Chung Yeung Festival is close at hand.

As the custom goes, all my brothers will climb a mountain and on the top they stand,

When dogwood sprays are shared out among them, that all but one are there they're sure to find.

别董大·其一

唐　高适

千里黄云白日曛，

北风吹雁雪纷纷。

莫愁前路无知己，

天下谁人不识君。

The First *Adieu to Dong Da, My Friend*

Yellowish clouds dimmed the sun and masked the whole sky,

Snowflakes were dancing to the north wind when to the south the

wild geese began to fly.

Despite a long way ahead, you would never run short of

understanding ear and admiring eye,

For throughout the world had been established your reputation so

high.

13

别董大·其二

唐　高适

六翮飘飖私自怜，

一离京洛十余年。

丈夫贫贱应未足，

今日相逢无酒钱。

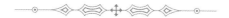

The Second *Adieu to Dong Da, My Friend*

Adrift hither and thither like a falling leaf, I was wallowing in a
slough of self-pity,

More than a decade had passed since my departure from Luoyang,
the capital city.

Despite the reluctance on a man's part to submit to poverty and
obscurity,

At our reunion that day, I couldn't even afford that small sum of
beer money.

除 夜 作

唐　高适

旅馆寒灯独不眠，

客心何事转凄然。

故乡今夜思千里，

霜鬓明朝又一年。

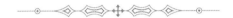

On New Year's Eve

At an inn, the candlelight flickered coldly yet I was accompanied by nothing but sleeplessness,

Suddenly came unsent for a fit of pain and sadness.

Though separated afar, my families must be missing me tonight, a moment of reunion happiness,

Tomorrow would mark the beginning of a new year when my hair was to grey even worse despite my unwillingness.

望庐山瀑布

唐 李白

日照香炉生紫烟，

遥看瀑布挂前川。

飞流直下三千尺，

疑是银河落九天。

The Waterfall of Mount Lu

Xianglu Summit is veiled by churning mist tinged purple in the sunlight,

Clinging to the face of a distant mountain is a waterfall with its sheer drop such an impressive sight.

As if rushing down from quite a great height,

It gives me a delusion that the Milky Way has come a long way across the space only to end up standing there upright.

赠 汪 伦

唐　李白

李白乘舟将欲行，

忽闻岸上踏歌声。

桃花潭水深千尺，

不及汪伦送我情。

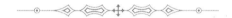

For Wang Lun, My Dear Friend

Having boarded a ship, I was all but ready for a journey,

Then and there someone came singing along the bank to me, his

steps to the beat of a melody.

It was said that the Peach−blossom Pond was deep unfathomably,

But not deep enough to hold our friendship, and with it Wang Lun

had come all the way to see me off purposely.

黄鹤楼送孟浩然之广陵

唐 李白

故人西辞黄鹤楼，

烟花三月下扬州。

孤帆远影碧空尽，

唯见长江天际流。

Seeing off Meng Haoran for
Yangzhou at Yellow–crane Tower

A friend eastward bound was waving farewell to me at the Yellow–crane Tower,

He was leaving for Yangzhou in March when the misty spring landscape was in full flower.

The lonely boat sailing far was diminishing before disappearing beneath the azure,

Within sight was nothing but the waters rolling forward into a distance beyond measure.

早发白帝城

唐　李白

朝辞白帝彩云间，

千里江陵一日还。

两岸猿声啼不住，

轻舟已过万重山。

Departure from Baidi City at Dawn

At dawn I left Baidi City with rosy clouds floating over,

Jiangling my destination far away was about a day's trip by water.

The woods on both sides were reverberating to monkeys' ceaseless chatter,

My boat was sailing swiftly, fleeting past one mountain after another.

望天门山

唐 李白

天门中断楚江开，

碧水东流至此回。

两岸青山相对出，

孤帆一片日边来。

In Admiration of Mount Tianmen

Mount Tianmen split apart where the Yangtze River was running through,

Here to the north the green waters rolling eastward were about to slew.

On both sides were mountains standing in symmetry and with lushly green trees they grew,

A boat came drifting into sight from out of an expanse of glowing blue.

20

题北榭碑

唐　李白

一为迁客去长沙，

西望长安不见家。

黄鹤楼中吹玉笛，

江城五月落梅花。

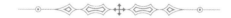

A Poem Inscribed on the Beixie Stele

History witnessed the banishment of the talented Jia Yi to Changsha, a remote city,

Looking westward into the distance, he knew that Changan was for ever out of his reach, and so was his family.

Then over the Yellow—crane Tower were lingering flute notes dripping with melancholy,

Sounding like the tune, the *Falling Plum Blossoms,* he was bound to feel a chill in the warm May beside the River Yangtze.

客中行

唐 李白

兰陵美酒郁金香，

玉碗盛来琥珀光。

但使主人能醉客，

不知何处是他乡。

A Sojourn on a Foreign Land

Wine made in Lanling County smells of distinctive turmeric aroma,

Brimmed with it, the transparent bowl is glazing like amber.

As a guest, I'm sure to be intoxicated for the hospitable host has

stood me to this best nectar,

Tipsy, I do feel at home where I'm none other than a newcomer.

闻王昌龄左迁龙标遥有此寄

唐 李白

杨花落尽子规啼，

闻道龙标过五溪。

我寄愁心与明月，

随风直到夜郎西。

For Wang Changling,
a Demoted and Banished Friend

Cuckoos' crow heralded the end of spring when willow catkins were littering the ground,

Then came to me the message that as far as Wuxi you had gone beyond.

I prayed that the bright moon could relay to you my concern so profound,

Despite your banishment to Yelang County in the far west, with you my solicitude would for ever stay around.

从军行·其二

唐　李白

百战沙场碎铁衣，

城南已合数重围。

突营射杀呼延将，

独领残兵千骑归。

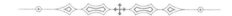

The Second *An Episode of War*

The general had survived hundreds of fierce battles, but not his armor,

Retreat to the south was cut off because of the heavy siege his troops were under.

Despite that, they charged the enemy bravely and his arrow pierced a tough warrior,

A successful sally though, so bloody was the fight that all but a thousand of his men had been buried there for ever.

春夜洛城闻笛

唐　李白

谁家玉笛暗飞声，

散入春风满洛城。

此夜曲中闻折柳，

何人不起故园情。

Fluting over Luoyang at a Spring Night

Flute notes soft and melodious are coming from nowhere,

By dint of wind, it's floating on Luoyang's night air.

Sounding to me *Zheyangliu*, a familiar folk tune about love—

hate affair,

It has awakened men's reminiscences so tender and fair.

山中问答

唐　李白

问余何意栖碧山，

笑而不答心自闲。

桃花流水窅然去，

别有天地非人间。

An Exchange of Opinions on Seclusive Life in a Mountain

In response to a query why to green mountains I had retired,

Smiling, I said nothing, relishing the mental peace inspired.

Falling peach blossoms were drifting downstream to as far as they desired,

This fairyland on earth spoke volumes about what you had inquired.

戏 赠 杜 甫

唐　李白

饭颗山头逢杜甫，

顶戴笠子日卓午。

借问别来太瘦生，

总为从前作诗苦。

A Poetic Tease of Du Fu, My Friend

On Fanko Mountain my encounter with Du Fu was an impressive

sight,

He wore a large bamboo hat when the sun was, highest in the sky,

shining bright.

Our meet last time still fresh in my mind, you seemed to have lost

quite a weight overnight,

The culprit turned out poetic composition, and against it you must

have been putting up a bitter fight.

春 怨

唐 李白

白马金羁辽海东，

罗帷绣被卧春风。

落月低轩窥烛尽，

飞花入户笑床空。

A Lovelorn Woman

Astride a white horse with a golden headstall, her husband was
sent to garrison the remote Liaodong Peninsula,

The soft breeze a tender caress, she was sleeping alone in bed
despite the beddings of fine fiber.

The setting moon peeped through the shutters only to find an
outburning candle and a self-pitying woman in company with each
other,

Wind-borne flower petals drifted in and lingered around as if
teasing this lovelorn creature.

劝 学 诗

唐　颜真卿

三更灯火五更鸡，

正是男儿读书时。

黑发不知勤学早，

白首方悔读书迟。

In Persistent Pursuit of Studies

In the small hours before the crowing of a rooster,

A man is supposed to study harder than ever.

If you're not committed therein as a youngster,

You're bound to end up a rueful greybeard in the future.

绝　句

唐　杜甫

两个黄鹂鸣翠柳，

一行白鹭上青天。

窗含西岭千秋雪，

门泊东吴万里船。

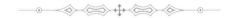

A Quatrain

Perching on a willow branch, two yellow orioles are chitchatting at leisure,

To the cloudless sky a row of white egrets is ascending in good order.

Through the window is brought into sight a lofty mountain with snow on top persisting for ever,

At a dock near my abode is anchoring a ship sailing all the way from southeastern China.

江南逢李龟年

唐　杜甫

岐王宅里寻常见，

崔九堂前几度闻。

正是江南好风景，

落花时节又逢君。

A Meet with Li Guinian,
a Famous Musician, South of Yangtze River

You used to execute beautiful music at Prince Qi's residence,

Also in the house of Cui Di, a high−ranking dignitary, your sweet singing was a frequent occurrence.

Now south of Yangtze River, the gorgeous landscape has established dominance,

Amid floating flowers, I've met you by a happy coincidence.

赠 花 卿

唐　杜甫

锦城丝管日纷纷，

半入江风半入云。

此曲只应天上有，

人间能得几回闻。

For Hua Jingding, an Assuming General

The city of Chengdu is resonating with a soft lingering melody,

By dint of wind, it's traveling upward through clouds or forward as
if to infinity.

So celestial is the music that it is otherwise composed exclusively
for the royal family,

What an arrogation that it's entertaining the plebeians
indiscriminately!

赠 李 白

唐　杜甫

秋来相顾尚飘蓬，

未就丹砂愧葛洪。

痛饮狂歌空度日，

飞扬跋扈为谁雄。

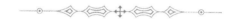

For Li Bai, My Friend

Tearing away from each other, we parted last autumn floating off
aimlessly,

Compared with Ge Hong, a well—known alchemist long ago, we
were both losers in striving for immortality.

In the indulgence of wine and song, you had let your years slip by
unknowingly,

For what on earth were you bearing yourself so defiantly?

江畔独步寻花·其五

唐 杜甫

黄师塔前江水东，

春光懒困倚微风。

桃花一簇开无主，

可爱深红爱浅红？

The Fifth *A Riverside Feast of Flowers*

Huangshi Tower is overlooking a river rolling eastward beyond horizon,

In the cozy spring breeze, a lassitude is taking hold of every person.

A constellation of peach blossoms is flourishing at full blast regardless of men's attention,

A salad of redness and pinkness, their loveliness is such as to arouse our endless admiration.

江畔独步寻花·其六

唐 杜甫

黄四娘家花满蹊，

千朵万朵压枝低。

留连戏蝶时时舞，

自在娇莺恰恰啼。

The Sixth *A Riverside Feast of Flowers*

Outside Mrs Huang's residence, the exuberance of flowers is such
as to hide the path they line from sight,
The branches are bowed down with countless flowers so bright.
Gravitating to their fragrance, butterflies are dancing leisurely with
delight,
Freewheeling orioles are singing merrily at a height.

绝句漫兴九首·其五

唐 杜甫

肠断江春欲尽头，

杖藜徐步立芳洲。

颠狂柳絮随风去，

轻薄桃花逐水流。

The Fifth of *A Collection of*
Nine Improvised Quatrains

Despite an exuberant sight, I sank into melancholy at the thought
of spring coming to an end,

I was hobbling along on a cane, and finally to a green–mantled
highland I strained to ascend.

Wafting away were the mindless willow catkins, and into the
distance they seemed to extend,

Flowing downstream were the fallen peach blossoms yielding
readily to whatever a trend.

绝句漫兴九首·其七

唐　杜甫

糁径杨花铺白毡，

点溪荷叶叠青钱。

笋根雉子无人见，

沙上凫雏傍母眠。

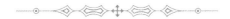

The Seventh of *A Collection of Nine Improvised Quatrains*

A path was bestrewed with a layer of willow catkins, such a white carpet,

Green lotus leaves were overlapping each other like stacked bronze coins, studding the surface of a rivulet.

Almost went unnoticed the bamboo shoots sprouting through the soil the smallest bit,

On a sandy beach was sleeping a newly−hatched duckling under mom's wing, quite a snug bed to it.

戏为六绝句·其一

唐 杜甫

庾信文章老更成，

凌云健笔意纵横。

今人嗤点流传赋，

不觉前贤畏后生。

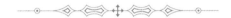

The First of *Six Quatrains*,
a Light-hearted Comment on Poetry

In old age, Yu Xin reached the zenith of his literary career,

In both content and style, he was a poet without peer.

But it is at his works that today's nobodies indulge in laugh and
jeer,

They're so presumptuous that should the great master come to life
again, their abuses might strike into him awe or even fear.

少 年 行

唐 杜甫

马上谁家薄媚郎，

临阶下马坐人床。

不通姓字粗豪甚，

指点银瓶索酒尝。

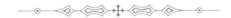

A Foppish Son

Astride on a high horse was a foppish son from some rich and
powerful family,

Dismounting at other's doorsteps, he barged in and dropped on
bed, all with his usual audacity.

This ill-bred dandy didn't even have his name announced, an
obvious breach of propriety,

For something to drink, he pointed to a silver jar, demanding the
host to make the wine ready.

逢入京使

唐　岑参

故园东望路漫漫，

双袖龙钟泪不干。

马上相逢无纸笔，

凭君传语报平安。

A Meet with an Envoy to the Capital

Forging further into the west, I looked back to the capital, my
hometown, now a far distant place,

Both ends of my sleeves were wet through after drying with them
the tears on my face.

Both astride on horses, we met on the way when writing a letter an
impossible case,

The envoy agreed to send my family a verbal message of my safety,
with a good grace.

枫 桥 夜 泊

唐　张继

月落乌啼霜满天，

江枫渔火对愁眠。

姑苏城外寒山寺，

夜半钟声到客船。

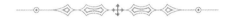

One Night's Stay on a Boat

At a frosty night, the moon is setting in the chorus of many a crow,

Beside a maple has anchored our ship where I'm staying up in

sorrow by the fisherman's candle with a dull glow.

From the Hanshan Temple in the suburb of Soochow,

The bell's toll at midnight is wafting to me, a man in spirits quite

low.

早 梅

唐 张渭

一树寒梅白玉条，

迥临村路傍溪桥。

不知近水花先发，

疑是经冬雪未销。

An Early-bloomed Plum Tree

Each branch a white-jade belt, a plum tree has burst into blossom
in defiance of coldness,

Far off the village road, it is seen beside a bridge on a rivulet,
standing with aloofness.

It has bloomed earlier thanks to its access to water nearby, yet to
everyone an obliviousness,

In their preconception, it is still snow-clad, a look consistent with
its winter usualness.

征 人 怨

唐　柳中庸

岁岁金河复玉关，

朝朝马策与刀环。

三春白雪归青冢，

万里黄河绕黑山。

War−weary Soldiers

Year after year, soldiers are fortifying the frontiers, east and west,

Day after day, they're weapons in hand and horses standby, going
on campaigns with barely any time to rest.

Despite the late spring, snow still frequents the northern grassland
and forest,

Beside the Yellow River or atop the Black Mountain, crusading
against the enemy they're doing their best.

春思二首·其一

唐 贾至

草色青青柳色黄，

桃花历乱李花香。

东风不为吹愁去，

春日偏能惹恨长。

The First *Recollections on a Spring Day*

Fresh grass was beckoning and yellowish leaves were sprouting
from willows, both flourishing under spring's tender care,

Peach trees were blazing with flowers and plum blossoms were
scenting the air.

Yet my sorrow remained unrelenting despite the loving spring
breeze everywhere,

And my bitterness kept breeding in a season so soft and fair.

重送裴郎中贬吉州

唐 刘长卿

猿啼客散暮江头，
人自伤心水自流。
同作逐臣君更远，
青山万里一孤舟。

Seeing off a Banished Friend

From afar came the whimper of monkeys when we parted against
the setting sun slightly above the river,
My sorrow was persisting, not even diluted a bit by the ever-
running water.
Both demoted, we were banished yet you to a place much farther,
Sailing beyond the green mountain ahead on a boat, you were still
to have endless miles to cover.

滁 州 西 涧

唐 韦应物

独怜幽草涧边生，

上有黄鹂深树鸣。

春潮带雨晚来急，

野渡无人舟自横。

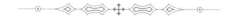

A Stream in the Western Suburb of Chuzhou

Grass thriving along a stream enchants me in particular,

In the depth of a leafy tree perches an oriole singing at leisure.

One night's rain begets a spring flood of surging water,

At a deserted ferry is seen a rolling boat at anchor.

春 怨

唐 刘方平

纱窗日落渐黄昏，

金屋无人见泪痕。

寂寞空庭春欲晚，

梨花满地不开门。

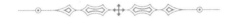

A Lovelorn Lady

At dusk, the sun is relenting outside the screened window,

In the harem is sobbing a fair lady in bitter sorrow.

The deserted courtyard sees the fading of spring about to die

tomorrow,

Pear blossoms littering the ground, she's locked in this golden

cage, worn by loneliness almost to a shadow.

夜上受降城闻笛

唐 李益

回乐峰前沙似雪，

受降城外月如霜。

不知何处吹芦管，

一夜征人尽望乡。

A Nostalgic Night at the Frontier

Mount Huile was overlooking an expanse of desert cold and white,

Above the Shouxiang Fortress was hanging an unfeeling moon, quite a frosty sight.

From nowhere was wafting up a reed whistling, a tune with a strong nostalgic bite,

For all conscripts, it meant a budding homesickness to ignite.

题鹤林寺僧舍

唐 李涉

终日昏昏醉梦间，
忽闻春尽强登山。
因过竹院逢僧话，
又得浮生半日闲。

A Poem Inscribed to Holin Temple

For a long time, I had been wasting my life in a fuddle,

One day I pulled myself together for mountain climbing since what

remained of the spring was very little.

I came across a monk, and with him I exchanged ideas, when I was

touring around a temple,

Half a day of leisure raced by when I put aside all worldly trouble.

金 缕 衣

唐 杜秋娘

劝君莫惜金缕衣，

劝君惜取少年时。

花开堪折直须折，

莫待无花空折枝。

A Gold−thread Robe

Into insignificance pales a gold−thread robe costly and stately,

Beside youthfulness passing fleetingly and irretrievably.

To break off a twig when flowers are blooming proves an action timely,

Should timing be wrong, you would get a stark branch barely.

洛 桥 晚 望

唐　孟郊

天津桥下冰初结，

洛阳陌上人行绝。

榆柳萧疏楼阁闲，

月明直见嵩山雪。

Night View of Luoyang

The Tianjin Bridge spanned a barely–frozen river,

Not far off, Luoyang saw the fading of pedestrians on all streets,

minor and major.

Behind the stark branches of elms and willows were empty

pavilions and lifeless mansions comprising a desolate picture,

On a bright moonlit night, the snow–mantled Mount Song afar was

visible in particular.

登科后

唐 孟郊

昔日龌龊不足夸，

今朝放荡思无涯。

春风得意马蹄疾，

一日看尽长安花。

At the Peak of My Life

I used to fall prey to failures and frustrations, now both having
paled into insignificance,

Having distinguished myself in the royal examination, I did feel
unchained, bursting with pride and confidence.

Flowers unfolding to greet spring, I was galloping lightly along
Changan's street, a sea of colorfulness and fragrance,

A day had flashed by when I was feasting my eyes on this realm of
iridescence.

城 东 早 春

唐　杨巨源

诗家清景在新春，

绿柳才黄半未匀。

若待上林花似锦，

出门俱是看花人。

Early Spring Scenery East of the Capital City

A poet is especially inspired by the early spring scenery,

The most typical proves the willows bursting into new leaves,

yellow and green mixed unevenly.

When the Capital turns into a sea of flowers as exquisite as those

on a piece of fine embroidery,

The admirers will be seen roaming everywhere in the city.

题都城南庄

唐　崔护

去年今日此门中，

人面桃花相映红。

人面不知何处去，

桃花依旧笑春风。

A Poem Inscribed to
a Manor House South of the Capital

On a spring day last year and right in this mansion,

I was admiring gorgeous peach blossoms, and suddenly of a fair maid I caught a vision.

One year later, I tried in vain to rediscover that pretty face when I revisited this place of fascination,

In the gentle breeze were still blooming the flowers in profusion.

十五夜望月

唐　王建

中庭地白树栖鸦，

冷露无声湿桂花。

今夜月明人尽望，

不知秋思落谁家。

Mid–Autumn Moon

Moonlight silvered the courtyard with an entourage of trees, a home to birds snugging in their respective nest,

Cold dewdrops softly moistened osmanthus blossoms, a peaceful picture to suggest.

That night, everyone was admiring the bright moon with zest,

However, it was laden with profound autumnal associations few people could digest.

海 人 谣

唐 王建

海人无家海里住，

采珠役象为岁赋。

恶波横天山塞路，

未央宫中常满库。

The Distressful

Homeless, he seeks a livelihood on the sea, the boat his only shelter,

For annual taxes and levies, he has to dive for pearls and hunt for ivories without a moment's leisure.

He cannot but work hard although in front of him may be awaiting a huge wave, an insurmountable mountain or whatever,

As a result, the emperor's treasury is bursting with gold and silver.

秋 思

唐 张籍

洛阳城里见秋风，

欲作家书意万重。

复恐匆匆说不尽，

行人临发又开封。

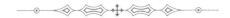

Nostalgic Autumn

Autumn wind was sweeping across the Luoyang city,

I was writing a letter to send my tender yet deep solicitude for my
family.

To make sure I had put my mind into words completely,

Before the messenger set off, I had opened the envelope to make a
second scrutiny.

早春呈水部张十八员外 / 初春小雨 / 早春

唐　韩愈

天街小雨润如酥，

草色遥看近却无。

最是一年春好处，

绝胜烟柳满皇都。

Early Spring

Steady rain was falling, nourishing everything on the streets of the Capital,

From afar the grass looked an expanse of greenness, yet around you it was but fractional.

Throughout a year, the present was the most beautiful, and with its arrival,

The spring charm had culminated, outshining the coming season when willows would burst into leaves and take on a misty look in the drizzle.

春 雪

唐 韩愈

新年都未有芳华，

二月初惊见草芽。

白雪却嫌春色晚，

故穿庭树作飞花。

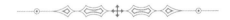

Spring Snow

Despite the advent of the first lunar month, flowers were late in
blooming,

One month later, I found to my surprise that grass was barely
sprouting.

Snow lingered on, as if pressing the spring for coming,

Between trees in the yard was raised a veil of snowflakes dancing.

晚　春

唐　韩愈

草树知春不久归，

百般红紫斗芳菲。

杨花榆荚无才思，

惟解漫天作雪飞。

Late Spring

As if knowing spring is drawing to the end,

Trees and flowers are in full bloom, and in beauty and fragrance they contend.

Even the unassuming catkins of willows and elms are straining to adapt to this trend,

Like snowflakes, they're dancing in the air and beyond the horizon they extend.

湘　中

唐　韩愈

猿愁鱼踊水翻波，
自古流传是汨罗。
蘋藻满盘无处奠，
空闻渔父扣舷歌。

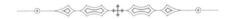

The Miluo River

Fish keeps leaping and diving the surging waters, and in the air is reverberating monkeys' whimper,

This is the Miluo River where for ages has long been passed down the story of the patriotic Quyuan drowning himself a martyr.

Not sure of the exact place of his death to pay tribute, I can not but conceive of those floating weeds as sacrifices to offer,

The folk song of a fisherman is wafting up across the river.

白 云 泉

唐　白居易

天平山上白云泉，

云自无心水自闲。

何必奔冲山下去，

更添波浪向人间。

White–cloud Spring

Halfway up Mount Tianping was a spring named White Cloud,

The water was at peace within, while the clouds crowning the top

were at ease without.

My White Cloud, I would rather you went anywhere but downhill

to spout,

For the world below was already overburdened with a dense and

turbulent crowd.

邯郸冬至夜思家

唐 白居易

邯郸驿里逢冬至，

抱膝灯前影伴身。

想得家中夜深坐，

还应说著远行人。

A Nostalgic Night at Handan

The day I spent at an inn in Handan happened to be midwinter,
otherwise an occasion for reuniting with my family,
Sitting hands on laps by candlelight, I had nothing but my shadow
for company.
That night, all my kins must be staying up together in delightful
harmony,
Quite likely they were talking about me, a son far away from his
native country.

采 莲 曲

唐　白居易

菱叶萦波荷飐风，

荷花深处小船通。

逢郎欲语低头笑，

碧玉搔头落水中。

A Lotus–gathering Song

Clinging to the water surface were the leaves of lotuses and water chestnuts, all in a breeze swaying,

Through the dense vegetations was sailing a small boat, and on it a maid was paddling.

Her lover coming into sight, she stopped just short of greeting him in others' presence, yet instead she lowered her head smiling,

However, a jade hair clasp slid off her hair and into the water apropos of nothing.

后 宫 词

唐　白居易

泪湿罗巾梦不成，

夜深前殿按歌声。

红颜未老恩先断，

斜倚薰笼坐到明。

Miserable Harem

Tears soaking her handkerchief, she was awake in bed yearning for the emperor's company,

Midnight though, from the front court still came the singing to the rhythm of a melody.

Still a pretty face though, already in disfavor was this fair lady,

She could not but sit beside an incense burner till daybreak, bleak and lonely.

暮 江 吟

唐　白居易

一道残阳铺水中，

半江瑟瑟半江红。

可怜九月初三夜，

露似真珠月似弓。

A River against the Setting Sun

The setting sun was glowing in the river,

Of redness and greenness was produced a mixture.

At an agreeable night on the third day of September,

On pearl–like dewdrops the bow–like moon was shedding luster.

大林寺桃花

唐　白居易

人间四月芳菲尽，

山寺桃花始盛开。

长恨春归无觅处，

不知转入此中来。

Peach Blossoms in Dalin Temple

In a world where most flowers have faded away in April,

Peach trees are just bursting into blossom in a highland temple.

While sighing over the bygone spring beyond retrieval,

I find to my surprise that time here seems to be standing still.

观 游 鱼

唐　白居易

绕池闲步看鱼游，

正值儿童弄钓舟。

一种爱鱼心各异，

我来施食尔垂钩。

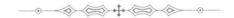

For the Sake of Fish

I was roaming around a pond, entertained by the fish swimming at ease,

Right then a boy was busy on a boat, attending to the fishing needs.

Both for the sake of this lovely creature, we were to do different deeds,

That's to say, he would set baits yet I give feeds.

咏 菊

唐　白居易

一夜新霜著瓦轻，

芭蕉新折败荷倾。

耐寒唯有东篱菊，

金粟初开晓更清。

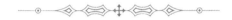

Chrysanthemums

Overnight the first frost descended on everything, and roof tiles
were covered with a layer very thin,

In consequence were drooped or broken the lotus and the plantain.

At a cold—resistance match among flowers, only the chrysanthemum
was sure to win,

Its newly—unfolded golden petals were especially refined and
fragrant when a new day was to begin.

鹅 赠 鹤

唐　白居易

君因风送入青云，

我被人驱向鸭群。

雪颈霜毛红网掌，

请看何处不如君？

A Goose's Complaint to a Crane

By dint of wind, you're soaring above clouds high,

Herded to flock with ducks, over that I cannot but sigh.

My feather being white, neck graceful and webbed feet bright red,

it is in any aspect that with you I'm qualified to vie,

Is it the God's will that I'm down here in the mud yet you're up

there in the sky?

浪 淘 沙

唐　白居易

白浪茫茫与海连，

平沙浩浩四无边。

暮去朝来淘不住，

遂令东海变桑田。

Impact of Waves upon a Sandy Beach

Swelling up from under the sea, waves are surging against the

shore, white—foaming,

Beyond eyeshot the smooth beach is extending.

Day and night, this swash seems for ever ongoing,

In a distant future, the change will be such as to transform this

place into a fertile field where mulberry trees are thriving.

望 洞 庭

唐　刘禹锡

湖光秋月两相和，

潭面无风镜未磨。

遥望洞庭山水翠，

白银盘里一青螺。

In Admiration of the Dongting Lake

The lake sparkles in the moonlight, calling to mind a harmonious
sight,

Without wind, the motionless water surface resembles a mirror
quite bright.

The emerald lake embraces a verdant mountain of lofty height,

Like a silver tray, on which a conch stands upright.

竹 枝 词

唐 刘禹锡

杨柳青青江水平，

闻郎江上踏歌声。

东边日出西边雨，

道是无晴却有晴。

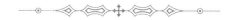

Romantic Delicacy

With an entourage of green trees, the river is flowing smoothly,

Then and there a lad comes singing along the bank to me, his steps

to the beat of a melody.

Around this time of a year, rain comes and goes unpredictably,

Though not a sunny day, my inner world starts shining affectionately.

乌 衣 巷

唐　刘禹锡

朱雀桥边野草花，

乌衣巷口夕阳斜。

旧时王谢堂前燕，

飞入寻常百姓家。

Wuyi Street

Around the Zhuque Bridge, weeds ran rampant and flowers went to seed,

The sunset glow fell aslant on the Wuyi Street, once the most prosperous yet now desolate indeed.

In the old days, it was a colony of dignitaries, also a choice for swallows to nest and breed,

Presently but a plebeian community, still a home to meet the birds' every need.

浪 淘 沙

唐 刘禹锡

九曲黄河万里沙，

浪淘风簸自天涯。

如今直上银河去，

同到牵牛织女家。

Impact of Waves upon a Sandy Beach

The Yellow River winds its way from afar, an enormous amount of
sand carried in its water,

Surging up and rolling forward, it seems to rush into an endless
vista.

Sometimes it rises up steeply to such a height that the Milky Way
looks just around the corner,

Perhaps it intends a visit to the Altair and the Vega, two stars each
epitomizing a faithful lover.

秋 词

唐 刘禹锡

自古逢秋悲寂寥，

我言秋日胜春朝。

晴空一鹤排云上，

便引诗情到碧霄。

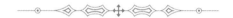

A Eulogy of Autumn

For most people, autumn evokes sadness or loneliness,

For me, it outshines spring in loveliness.

A crane is soaring up into the sky, an expanse of cloudlessness,

Likewise, my poetic inspirations break loose and reach upward to

infiniteness.

与浩初上人同看山寄京华亲故

唐　柳宗元

海畔尖山似剑铓，

秋来处处割愁肠。

若为化得身千亿，

散上峰头望故乡。

In Remembrance of
my Family in the Distant Capital

Not far from the sea rises a train of mountain peaks as sharp as the
tip of a saber,

In autumn especially, they seem to exacerbate my homesickness
as an impressive reminder,

Should there be a spell turning me from one into quite a number,

Each ascends to one top and looks into my distant hometown,
praying for family reunion over and over.

柳州二月榕叶落尽偶题

唐 柳宗元

宦情羁思共凄凄，

春半如秋意转迷。

山城过雨百花尽，

榕叶满庭莺乱啼。

A Poem Improvised in February at Liuzhou, a Place of Fallen Leaves

Politically crossed, I was banished far away from my family, therefore overcome with bitterness,

For me, the mid-spring flourishing sight was as depressing as that of late autumn, contributing nothing to pull me out of wretchedness.

In this remote mountain area, a burst of rain had faded all flowers giving way to listlessness,

Fallen banyan leaves littering the courtyard, the chirping of orioles simply added to my irksomeness.

酬王二十舍人雪中见寄

唐　柳宗元

三日柴门拥不开，

阶平庭满白皑皑。

今朝蹋作琼瑶迹，

为有诗从凤沼来。

Reading a Friend's Poem in Snow

For days has been locked the door of my humble residence,

Its courtyard and doorsteps are covered with a blanket of snow in

consequence.

Like a jade broken into pieces, this white sheet has turned chaotic

with messy footsteps spoiling its intact existence,

For I can't help pacing up and down in excitement while reading a

poem sent from the Capital in the farthest distance.

重别梦得

唐　柳宗元

二十年来万事同，

今朝岐路忽西东。

皇恩若许归田去，

晚岁当为邻舍翁。

A Second Farewell to Liu Yuxi, My Dear Friend

In the past twenty years, we both have gone through the vicissitudes of fate,

Today at this crossroads we again have to separate.

Should one day His Majesty be kind enough to relieve me of my official weight,

After retirement, I would have my residence next to yours locate.

离思五首·其四

唐　元稹

曾经沧海难为水，

除却巫山不是云。

取次花丛懒回顾，

半缘修道半缘君。

The Fourth *Lovesickness*

Other waters are nothing but a pool compared to the boundless sea,

No clouds are more gorgeous than those floating over Mount Wu free.

I am fleeting through beautiful flowers irresistible to anyone else but me,

Partly because of self-restraint and mostly of unforgettable thee.

小 儿 垂 钓

唐　胡令能

蓬头稚子学垂纶，

侧坐莓苔草映身。

路人借问遥招手，

怕得鱼惊不应人。

A Fishing Child

A child is learning fishing, his hair disheveled in a breeze,

Squatting on a mossy stone, he is half hidden behind weeds.

Waving hastily to hush a passer-by, the boy sits in a freeze,

He remains his lips sealed lest fish might flee in stampedes.

南园十三首·其五

唐 李贺

男儿何不带吴钩，

收取关山五十州。

请君暂上凌烟阁，

若个书生万户侯？

Sighing over My Fate

More than anything else does, a saber becomes a man of aspiration,

Weapon in hand, he's set to recover the vast land under enemy occupation.

Of the twenty-four Founding Fathers worshipped in the National Hall of Commemoration,

Most of them are granted the highest-ranking peerage on the strength of their military merit rather than scholarly erudition.

泊 秦 淮

唐 杜牧

烟笼寒水月笼沙，

夜泊秦淮近酒家。

商女不知亡国恨，

隔江犹唱后庭花。

One Night on the Qinhuai River

Rolling gently were the misty and cold waters of Qinhuai River,

and the white sands alongside were shimmering in the moonlight,

My boat was pulling into a river-side tavern when gradually fell

the night.

For singing girls, the perished kingdom had long been fading out

of sight,

Their business was to entertain the visitors by singing soft and

effeminate songs with delight.

山 行

唐　杜牧

远上寒山石径斜，

白云生处有人家。

停车坐爱枫林晚，

霜叶红于二月花。

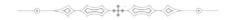

Up a Mountain

Along a winding path, I made my way up a mountain in the autumn coldness,

A few households were scattered on the top nestling in a mist of whiteness.

I pulled over my cart to feast my eyes on the maples against the gathering darkness,

Hardened by frost, their leaves outshone February flowers in redness.

清 明

唐 杜牧

清明时节雨纷纷，

路上行人欲断魂。

借问酒家何处有？

牧童遥指杏花村。

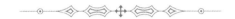

Tomb–sweeping Day

A persistent drizzle was falling around the Tomb–sweeping Day,

Passers–by on every street looked sad and grey.

I inquired the whereabouts of a tavern where for wine I might have

a short stay,

A shepherd boy pointed to the Apricot–blossom Village a distance

away.

江 南 春

唐　杜牧

千里莺啼绿映红，

水村山郭酒旗风。

南朝四百八十寺，

多少楼台烟雨中。

A Spring Sight South of the Yangtze River

Before us is unrolled an ever–extending landscape where birds fly
singing above green trees and red flowers,
In waterside villages and hill–foot towns, tavern banners are
billowed by wind with all its powers.
Across the Southern Kingdoms are standing hundreds of temples
and towers,
All taking on a misty look in fitful showers.

秋 夕

唐 杜牧

银烛秋光冷画屏，

轻罗小扇扑流萤。

天阶夜色凉如水，

卧看牵牛织女星。

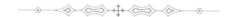

An Autumn Night

At an autumn night, a chill was hanging over a painted screen under that silver of moon and candle,

A court maid was, a gauze fan in hand, chasing a firefly to amuse hours monotonous and idle.

Though inside the palace was sleeping everything as cold as marble,

The girl was reposing on a stone step, gazing at the Altair and the Vega, a double star symbolizing a faithful and unseparated couple.

赠 别

唐 杜牧

多情却似总无情，

唯觉樽前笑不成。

蜡烛有心还惜别，

替人垂泪到天明。

A Parting Poem as a Keepsake

Both impressible, we just sat speechless, striking each other as
being unfeeling,

Proposing her a toast, I forced in vain to present a face smiling.

The candle flickered knowingly, as if in lamentation of our parting,

Guttering nonstop, it was like shedding tears for us until the first
light of next morning.

叹 花

唐 杜牧

自是寻春去校迟，

不须惆怅怨芳时。

狂风落尽深红色，

绿叶成阴子满枝。

Sighing over Flowers

It was my fault to go spring outing late when most blossoms had
worn away,

A pity though, I knew that florescence was not something one
could delay.

Flowers would fade in autumn wind, come what may,

Then trees would be heavy with fruits and take on a fresh green
look on the coming harvest day.

南 陵 道 中

唐　杜牧

南陵水面漫悠悠，

风紧云轻欲变秋。

正是客心孤迥处，

谁家红袖凭江楼？

On My Way to Nanling County

Water brimmed Nanling River rolling on at leisure,

Rising wind and pale clouds foreboded that autumn was just around the corner.

Far away from home, I felt lonely and rather gloomy about my future,

Then and there came into sight a fair maid beside an attic window in a sitting posture.

题乌江亭

唐 杜牧

胜败兵家事不期，
包羞忍耻是男儿。
江东子弟多才俊，
卷土重来未可知。

A Poem Inscribed on Wujiang Pavilion
to Mark Xiang Yu's Death

Battle-wise, victory and defeat are more often than not unpredictable,

He who is able to survive a disgraceful fiasco will end up a man truly invincible.

Southeastern China proves the cradle of heroes most remarkable,

Should Xiang Yu, the lord of Kingdom Chu, not kill himself in response to a humiliating defeat, a comeback would be by no means impossible.

过 分 水 岭

唐　温庭筠

溪水无情似有情，

入山三日得同行。

岭头便是分头处，

惜别潺湲一夜声。

Parting

The unfeeling rivulet means to me a dear friend,

She has been keeping my company through the mountain for three

days on end.

The top over there is where to different directions we'll descend,

Unwilling to part with her, that night to her sweet murmurs I've

been staying up to attend.

陇 西 行

唐　陈陶

誓扫匈奴不顾身，

五千貂锦丧胡尘。

可怜无定河边骨，

犹是春闺梦里人！

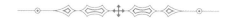

The North—western Frontier

Determined to vanquish the enemy, our soldiers charged the Huns
disregardful of their own safety,

Well—equipped and battle—seasoned though, five thousand men
fell in the nomadic territory.

Their bodies already scattered bones along the Wuding River,
what a tragedy!

Not knowing what had become of her husband, a wife was still
dreaming of him back to the family.

夜雨寄北

唐　李商隐

君问归期未有期，

巴山夜雨涨秋池。

何当共剪西窗烛，

却话巴山夜雨时。

A Letter to My Beloved
in the North at a Rainy Night

It was hard to tell when I could return to your side,

All rivers and lakes around Mount Ba had brimmed after a night's

heavy rain refusing to subside.

I was yearning for the day when the candlelight would project our

silhouettes on the window, and when never again would we divide,

Then in you I would affectionately confide.

为 有

唐 李商隐

为有云屏无限娇，

凤城寒尽怕春宵。

无端嫁得金龟婿，

辜负香衾事早朝。

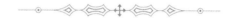

For What She Bemoans

A graceful beauty is seated behind a screen with exquisite carving,

The freezing winter is drawing to an end in the Capital where spring night turns out something mind–disturbing.

For all you know, she has, of all things, married an official high–ranking,

He has to leave early for the imperial court, tearing himself away from his wife so charming.

霜 月

唐　李商隐

初闻征雁已无蝉，

百尺楼高水接天。

青女素娥俱耐冷，

月中霜里斗婵娟。

Frost and Moon

Cicadas have stopped humming when southbound wild geese fly

honking across the sky,

From the top of a high building, I look into the distance where the

distinctions between heaven and earth are blurred in my eye.

It is said that for the two fairies, Qingnv and Chang'e, coldness is

the first thing they defy,

One the goddess of frost and the other of moon, in beauty and

grace they'll never cease to vie.

暮秋独游曲江

唐　李商隐

荷叶生时春恨生，

荷叶枯时秋恨成。

深知身在情长在，

怅望江头江水声。

Beside the Qu River in Late Autumn

Lotus leaves were sprouting in spring when I slid into weariness,

They withered in autumn when I struggled in vain to get over this passiveness.

Love would never die before life met its end, a belief I had been living by with full awareness,

The river seemed running on exhaustless, and so was my melancholiness.

端 居

唐　李商隐

远书归梦两悠悠，

只有空床敌素秋。

阶下青苔与红树，

雨中寥落月中愁。

Affectionate Remembrances

I dreamed of reunion with my wife, from whom a letter was what I
had long been expecting,

Only to wake up alone in bed on a frosty autumn morning.

A red maple overshadowed my doorsteps, on which moss was
creeping,

The cold moon dimmed in the rain, and for my beloved I was
pining.

官 仓 鼠

唐 曹邺

官仓老鼠大如斗，

见人开仓亦不走。

健儿无粮百姓饥，

谁遣朝朝入君口。

Granary Mice

Corpulent mice were running rampant in the state granary,

Despite men's approaching, they remained where they were disregardfully.

When soldiers and civilians were starving as a result of grain scarcity,

They were feasting on people's flesh and blood unscrupulously.

咏架上鹰

唐 崔铉

天边心胆架头身，

欲拟飞腾未有因。

万里碧霄终一去，

不知谁是解绦人。

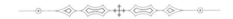

A Caged Eagle

His body was caged, but never his courage and pride,

He meant to break free, but opportunities were denied.

One day he would be soaring across the vast sky, yet his time he

had to bide,

The question was who would have his chain untied.

不第后赋菊

唐　黄巢

待到秋来九月八，

我花开后百花杀。

冲天香阵透长安，

满城尽带黄金甲。

Chrysanthemums for a Failed Examinee

By the eighth of the ninth lunar month this fall,

Chrysanthemums will be in full bloom while all others take a call.

Their fragrance will permeate every corner within the Capital's

wall,

And a golden sea of flowers will hold dominion over all.

题 菊 花

唐　黄巢

飒飒西风满院栽，

蕊寒香冷蝶难来。

他年我若为青帝，

报与桃花一处开。

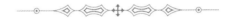

Chrysanthemums

The west wind rustled chrysanthemums in the garden on an autumn day,

The chill of their pistils and scents is such as to keep butterflies at bay.

Should one day I be the god holding sway,

I would advance their florescence to spring when with peach blossoms they would be both on display.

己亥岁感事

唐　曹松

泽国江山入战图，

生民何计乐樵苏。

凭君莫话封侯事，

一将功成万骨枯。

A Helpless Sigh

The battle map showed that the flames of war were searing many a
mountain and river,

People had subsisted barely by chopping wood or cutting grass,
but soon their scanty livelihood would be over.

For me, a peerage granted for military merit was the last thing I
would strive after,

For all you know, thousands of people might have died in exchange
for just one general's glory and honor.

蜂

唐　罗隐

不论平地与山尖，

无限风光尽被占。

采得百花成蜜后，

为谁辛苦为谁甜？

Bees

A plain or a highland, it doesn't matter,

Where there're blooming flowers, there're bees as busy as ever.

They've made it honey after numerous round trips to gather nectar,

One cannot help asking for what they're toiling and to whom

they're giving the sweet fruits of their labor.

自 遣

唐 罗隐

得即高歌失即休，

多愁多恨亦悠悠。

今朝有酒今朝醉，

明日愁来明日愁。

A Solace to Myself

You should seize the chance to chant aloud before it slips by,

Despite sorrows and regrets, you can sing to let your heart fly.

Wine accessible now, drink it up and make yourself high,

Tomorrow's annoyances are yet to come and not in today's eye.

咏 蟹

唐 皮日休

未游沧海早知名，

有骨还从肉上生。

莫道无心畏雷电，

海龙王处也横行。

A Crab

Having never been to the sea, a crab's home, I've long been aware of his reputation,

So weird—looking is he that his entire fleshy body is under shell's protection.

Defiant and fearless, he never flinches from thunder or lightning, a carrier of God's indignation,

Even in the presence of Poseidon, he advances crabwise without the slightest compunction.

焚 书 坑

唐 章碣

竹帛烟销帝业虚，

关河空锁祖龙居。

坑灰未冷山东乱，

刘项原来不读书。

Books Burnt to Ashes

The Emperor decreed the burning of all classics, a mandate that had undermined his empire's foundation,

The geographical advantages around his Capital failed to fend off the insurgents' aggression.

The embers were yet to die out while the eastern domain had been thrown into utter commotion,

For all you might know, Liu Bang and Xiang Yu, the top two rebel leaders, had never read any books, especially the Confucian.

台 城

唐 韦庄

江雨霏霏江草齐，

六朝如梦鸟空啼。

无情最是台城柳，

依旧烟笼十里堤。

Taicheng

In a steady drizzle, a fresh greenness was extending along the
Yangtze River,
To its south were once founded in succession six dynasties, a
dreamy past seen off in the birds' twitter.
In spite of everything, the willows overshadowing Taicheng, once
the site of the imperial palace, remained an indifferent on-looker,
They were still thriving on the long misty causeway as a historical
reminder.

金 陵 图

唐　韦庄

谁谓伤心画不成，

画人心逐世人情。

君看六幅南朝事，

老木寒云满故城。

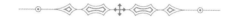

Six Paintings of Jinling City

Most paintings epitomize anything but sadness,

In that painters cater to the popular pursuit of happiness.

Please look at these six portraying the perished kingdoms with

their capitals all in Jin Ling, quite a historical witness,

Only to find dying trees and looming storms everywhere, such a

sight of gloominess.

再经胡城县

唐　杜荀鹤

去岁曾经此县城，

县民无口不冤声。

今来县宰加朱绂，

便是生灵血染成。

A Grief−stricken County

Early last year when I made my first stopover at this county,

All people there were wailing over the injustice imposed by

officials greedy and filthy.

Yesterday's local magistrate was then dressed in a red robe, a sign

of being promoted officially,

Also a witness to the tear and blood of those in misery.

蚕 妇

唐　杜荀鹤

粉色全无饥色加，

岂知人世有荣华。

年年道我蚕辛苦，

底事浑身着苎麻。

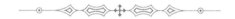

A Silkworm Keeper

A hungry look and a sallow complexion,

She was barely subsisting, an affluent life beyond her conception.

For silkworm rearing, she was all but prostrate with exhaustion,

Yet she wore but shabby clothes of hemp fiber, a fact without the

least justification.

自　遣

唐　杜苟鹤

粝食粗衣随分过，

堆金积帛欲如何。

百年身后一丘土，

贫富高低争几多。

A Solace to Myself

I'm content with coarse clothing and humble fare,
Heaps of gold and silk will simply get me nowhere.
For an alive, all but a small patch of resting−place prove a mortal affair,
For a dead, wealth and rank are out of his care.

鹭 鸶

唐 郑谷

闲立春塘烟淡淡，

静眠寒苇雨飕飕。

渔翁归后汀沙晚，

飞下滩头更自由。

Egrets

Spring mist descends a lake, and beside it is standing an egret at
leisure,

Sometimes he is reposing in a cove of reeds, heedless of the chilly
shower.

Fishermen having left, the sandy beach is fading in the darkness to
gather,

Now the birds are flying up and down here at ease and with
pleasure.

社 日

唐　王驾

鹅湖山下稻粱肥，

豚栅鸡栖半掩扉。

桑柘影斜春社散，

家家扶得醉人归。

Harvest Revelry

At the foot of Ehu Mountain, crops were coming on splendidly,

Everywhere was a picture of thriving livestock and poultry.

Shadows of trees were drawing out, and finally came the windup of
the harvest revelry,

The drunk were shambling home on the arm of their respective
family.

猿

唐　徐寅

宿有乔林饮有溪，

生来踪迹远尘泥。

不知心更愁何事，

每向深山夜夜啼。

Monkeys

Sleeping on trees, monkeys quench their thirst in a stream,

Shuttling high above the dusty world, they are held in high esteem.

Freewheeling and carefree though they seem,

Every night through the valley reverberates their whimper mingled

with scream.

农 父

唐 张碧

运锄耕劚侵星起，

陇亩丰盈满家喜。

到头禾黍属他人，

不知何处抛妻子。

An Old Peasant

Every morning he gets up by starlight, toiling and moiling in the
field for a whole day,

Now his family is rejoicing at a good harvest on its way.

Unfortunately, almost nothing belongs to him who has exorbitant
levies to pay,

He may one day sell his wife and children to survive this cruel
flay.

观 祈 雨

唐 李约

桑条无叶土生烟，

箫管迎龙水庙前。

朱门几处看歌舞，

犹恐春阴咽管弦。

Praying for Rain

A terrible drought was wreaking havoc, leaves falling off trees and
dust swirling in the air,

At a temple, people were drumming and gonging, pleading the
Rain God to show mercy and care.

Singing and dancing seemed ongoing in rich families everywhere,

For them, musical instruments rusting in dampness would be the
most annoying affair.

咏 蚕

唐　蒋贻恭

辛勤得茧不盈筐，

灯下缫丝恨更长。

著处不知来处苦，

但贪衣上绣鸳鸯。

A Silkworm Raiser

She was at pains to raise silkworms only to yield threads less than a basketful,

Reeling cocoons by candlelight, of injustice she was deeply resentful.

Those dressed in silk cared nothing about her life miserable and painful,

Their only concern was whether or not the mandarin ducks embroidered thereon were graceful and beautiful.

述 亡 国 诗

五代　花蕊夫人

君王城上竖降旗，

妾在深宫那得知？

十四万人齐解甲，

更无一个是男儿！

Lamentation over My Perished Kingdom

Raising a white flag, the king surrendered a walled city,

A woman confined in the harem, how could I know this tragedy?

One hundred and forty thousand soldiers had laid down their arms
quite ready,

Not a single one of them proved a man of courage and dignity.

清　明

宋　王禹偁

无花无酒过清明，

兴味萧然似野僧。

昨日邻家乞新火，

晓窗分与读书灯。

Qingming Festival

Without flowers and wines to greet the Qingming Festival,

I was as dull and austere as a monk in a desolate temple.

Yesterday I asked a favor of my neighbor for a kindling to warm up my home cold and humble,

Before daybreak, I started reading beside a window by a newly lit-up candle.

书河上亭壁

宋　寇准

岸阔樯稀波渺茫，

独凭危槛思何长。

萧萧远树疏林外，

一半秋山带夕阳。

A Poem Inscribed on the Wall of
a River–side Pavilion

Several ships were ploughing across the Yellow River, a vast expanse of misty and rolling waters,

To vent my pent–up sorrow, I ascended a pavilion and stood behind its banisters.

Far away, autumn wind was soughing through a scattering of poplars,

Against the setting sun, a mountain was half bathed in golden shimmers.

画 眉 鸟

宋　欧阳修

百啭千声随意移，

山花红紫树高低。

始知锁向金笼听，

不及林间自在啼。

Thrushes

Thrushes are singing melodiously, as delightful as they please,

Their songs are reverberating over colorful flowers blooming

between undulating trees.

Compared to those chirping in golden cages to meet people's

entertaining needs,

Birds in the woods are twittering with carefree ease.

别 滁

宋 欧阳修

花光浓烂柳轻明，

酌酒花前送我行。

我亦且如常日醉，

莫教弦管作离声。

Farewell to My People at Chuzhou

A day when flowers and willows are in their heyday,

I'm sipping at a send—off while around me the spring sights stay.

As usual, I'm intoxicated with fine wine and musical play,

However, I do hate the tune reminding me that soon I'll tear myself

away.

咏 柳
宋 曾巩

乱条犹未变初黄，

倚得东风势便狂。

解把飞花蒙日月，

不知天地有清霜。

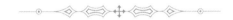

Willows

Willow twigs are intertwined, not yet turning yellowish-green,

Lashed by the east wind, rampantly swaying they've ever been.

Whirling catkins have overclouded the sun like a screen,

When a frost descends, they'll immediately be purged clean.

城 南

宋 曾巩

雨过横塘水满堤，

乱山高下路东西。

一番桃李花开尽，

惟有青青草色齐。

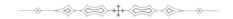

South of the Town

Water brims the Hengtang river after a heavy rain,

Far away extend undulating mountains with two paths, one to the

east and one the west, winding down the terrain.

While peach and plum blossoms are on the wane,

Still lushly green do the grasses remain.

书湖阴先生壁

宋　王安石

茅檐长扫净无苔，

花木成畦手自栽。

一水护田将绿绕，

两山排闼送青来。

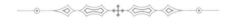

A Poem Inscribed on the Wall of Yang Ji's Cottage

A last place to gather moss, the courtyard is spotless thanks to frequent sweeping,

Trees and flowers are well trimmed and beautifully shaped, a result of the owner's careful tending.

Embraced and nourished by a river, the farmlands take on a look thriving,

A door flung open, a fresh lushness is coming to greet my eyes through two mountains each other confronting.

元　日

宋　王安石

爆竹声中一岁除，

春风送暖入屠苏。

千门万户曈曈日，

总把新桃换旧符。

New Year's Day

Firecrackers were set off to bang out the old year,

To see in the new, people drank Tusu wine when spring warmth

was drawing near.

High above thousands of households was the bright sun glowing in

top gear,

Old Spring Festival couplets were torn off every door to make room

for the new, a blessing for what were held dear.

泊 船 瓜 洲

宋　王安石

京口瓜洲一水间，

钟山只隔数重山。

春风又绿江南岸，

明月何时照我还？

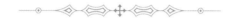

One Night's Stay on a Ship Anchored at Guazhou

Jingkou and Guazhou are at close range, separated by a narrow
strip of water,
Just a few mountains off is Zhongshan, the hometown I yearn after.
The gentle spring breeze has puffed everything green south of the
Yangtze River,
I pray to the bright moon for family reunion the sooner the better.

登飞来峰

宋　王安石

飞来山上千寻塔，

闻说鸡鸣见日升。

不畏浮云遮望眼，

只缘身在最高层。

On the Top of Mount Feilai

It's said that on the top of Mount Feilai stands a tower dizzily high,

There the sun rises in immediate response to a rooster's cry.

My eyes are blown open despite the floating clouds across the sky,

The top floor I've set foot on is why.

春 夜

宋　王安石

金炉香尽漏声残，

剪剪轻风阵阵寒。

春色恼人眠不得，

月移花影上栏杆。

A Spring Night

Incense is burning out in a golden censer and water dripping out
in a clepsydra,

Gusts of wind spell chills over and over.

I am rendered sleepless with spring sight such a bewitcher,

The moon swims in the sky, projecting flower shadows on the
balcony of a chamber.

钟山即事

宋　王安石

涧水无声绕竹流，

竹西花草弄春柔。

茅檐相对坐终日，

一鸟不鸣山更幽。

A Sightseeing Tour of Mount Zhong

A stream is looping around a bamboo grove noiselessly,

On its west, grasses and flowers are beckoning in the spring breeze

softly.

Under the eaves of my cottage, I prefer to sit out the day relishing

the beautiful scenery,

Birds have stopped chirping and everything in the valley is given a

touch of tranquility.

春 日 偶 成

宋　程颢

云淡风轻近午天，

傍花随柳过前川。

时人不识余心乐，

将谓偷闲学少年。

A Poem Improvised on a Spring Day

A cloudless and windless day, I was strolling out and unknowingly
the sun rose highest in the sky,

I wound through blossoms and willows before the path led me to a
river nearby.

Right then, my inner joy was such as to defy the perception of any
worldly eye,

In which I was, though old, seeking fun and leisure like a young
guy.

夏日登车盖亭

宋 蔡确

纸屏石枕竹方床，

手倦抛书午梦长。

睡起莞然成独笑，

数声渔笛在沧浪。

Under Chegai Pavilion on a Summer Day

Shaded by a papered screen, I was reading on a bamboo couch, reclining against a stone pillow,

Tired and putting aside the book, I was overcome with sleepiness and a good siesta to follow.

Waking up, I couldn't help smiling at the truth that the vicissitudes of life were all but a fleeting shadow,

Then above the Canglang River, a fisherman's whistle evoked a lingering echo.

惠崇春江晓景

宋　苏轼

竹外桃花三两枝，

春江水暖鸭先知。

蒌蒿满地芦芽短，

正是河豚欲上时。

A Poem Inscribed on the Painting *A Riverside Spring Morning*

Not far from a bamboo grove, sprays of peach blossoms are swaying in the breeze,

In spring, river water is warming up, a perceivable change for ducks swimming as they please.

Nearby, mugwort is thriving while putting forth are the shoots of reeds,

It's a time when blowfish migrates upstream and breeds.

题 西 林 壁

宋　苏轼

横看成岭侧成峰，

远近高低各不同。

不识庐山真面目，

只缘身在此山中。

A Poem Inscribed on the Wall of Xilin Temple

Mount Lu looks a ridge frontally, but a peak laterally,

With perspective varies its visage in size or proximity.

No eye can capture its full view in the reality,

An observer in the picture is the culprit of this visual anomaly.

六月二十七日望湖楼醉书

宋 苏轼

黑云翻墨未遮山，

白雨跳珠乱入船。

卷地风来忽吹散，

望湖楼下水如天。

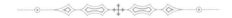

A Poem Composed in Tipsiness at
Wanghu Tower on June 27

Rolling pitch-dark clouds are yet to mask the mountain top,

Splashing on my boat is a heavy rain of many a pearl-like drop.

With the rising of a gusty wind, clouds disperse and the pour comes to an immediate stop,

Now the Wanghu Tower is overlooking a vast lake calming down quite a lot.

137

饮湖上初晴后雨二首·其一

宋　苏轼

朝曦迎客艳重冈，

晚雨留人入醉乡。

此意自佳君不会，

一杯当属水仙王。

The First *Sunny and Rainy Looks*
of the West Lake

Mountains were bathed in the red glow of dawn when I set off for a
meet with a friend,

In tipsiness, he fell asleep when a night drizzle began to descend.

After all, the gravity of the scene went unnoticed to him in the end,

Proposing a toast to the patron saint of the West Lake, I admired
its sunny and rainy looks in a perfect blend.

饮湖上初晴后雨二首·其二

宋 苏轼

水光潋滟晴方好，

山色空蒙雨亦奇。

欲把西湖比西子，

淡妆浓抹总相宜。

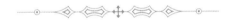

The Second *Sunny and Rainy Looks of the West Lake*

The glowing sun is shedding light on the rippling water,

In a drizzle, mountains take on a misty look with a unique flavor.

The appeal of the West Lake is such as to remind us of Xi Shi, a

peerless beauty in ancient China,

With a heavy makeup or a light one, she remains a belle of

dazzling luster.

春 宵

宋　苏轼

春宵一刻值千金，
花有清香月有阴。
歌管楼台声细细，
秋千院落夜沉沉。

A Spring Night

With every minute's worth a thousand pieces of gold, a spring night is a treasure almost invaluable,

The fragrance of flowers is lingering in the air, and the moon is shedding light on everything with a reflection faintly visible.

Over pavilions and terraces are floating singers' melodies sweet and gentle,

Darkness and peace descend a courtyard where a swing is staying idle.

海 棠

宋 苏轼

东风袅袅泛崇光，
香雾空蒙月转廊。
只恐夜深花睡去，
故烧高烛照红妆。

Flowering Crabapple

A gentle breeze from the east puffs the clouds away, unveiling a moon glowing faintly,

Through a mist of fragrance, the moon is seen swimming to the other side of the gallery.

For fear of missing its transient bloom in the midnight, though a fact of uncertainty,

I keep the candle burning and stay up for the arrival of the beauty.

牧 童 诗

宋 黄庭坚

骑牛远远过前村,

短笛横吹隔陇闻。

多少长安名利客,

机关用尽不如君。

A Cowherd Boy

Astride on a buffalo, he's roaming at large in front of a distant village,

Holding a piccolo laterally, he's playing a tune wafting up from across many a ridge.

Compared to those flocking to the Capital for fame, wealth or any privilege,

The boy never demeans himself by resorting to scheme or cozenage.

鄂州南楼书事

宋　黄庭坚

四顾山光接水光，

凭栏十里芰荷香。

清风明月无人管，

并作南楼一味凉。

Around the Nan Tower at Ezhou

Looking around, I'm admiring the green mountains and clear
waters making a perfect landscape picture,
Across the vast expanse of the lake are flourishing lotuses and
water caltrops, both with pleasant aroma.
The soft breeze and bright moon are still as at ease as ever,
Together they generate a refreshing coolness lingering in the Nan
Tower.

禾 熟

宋 孔平仲

百里西风禾黍香，

鸣泉落窦谷登场。

老牛粗了耕耘债，

啮草坡头卧夕阳。

Harvest

The west wind is holding sway, and over a vast expanse of farmland

permeates the scent of ripening crop,

Gurgling water running down canals and ditches, farmers are busy

threshing grain nonstop.

Most of the year being kept on the hop,

A buffalo is napping in the setting sun after browsing the hilltop.

春 日

宋 晁冲之

阴阴溪曲绿交加，

小雨翻萍上浅沙。

鹅鸭不知春去尽，

争随流水趁桃花。

A Spring Day

A winding brook flows through the shady canopy of lushly green
trees,

Like fine sand grains, falling raindrops are dancing on floating
duckweeds.

Spring has passed unnoticed to ducks and geese,

Chasing floating peach blossoms, they're frolicking at ease.

游园不值

宋 叶绍翁

应怜屐齿印苍苔，

小扣柴扉久不开。

春色满园关不住，

一枝红杏出墙来。

A Closed Garden Inaccessible to Visitors

With the misgiving that the moss-clad floor might fall victim to visitors' clogs, the owner has locked his garden's gate,

A few taps on the door produce no result, as I can anticipate.

In spite of everything, the enchantment of spring is not something one can incarcerate,

Over the wall, a spray of pink apricot blossoms has lolled out, right for me to appreciate.

夜书所见

宋 叶绍翁

萧萧梧叶送寒声，

江上秋风动客情。

知有儿童挑促织，

夜深篱落一灯明。

A Night Portrait

Leaves of plane-trees were rustling in the coldness,

Autumn wind swept across the river, awakening my homesickness.

Kids at home were conducting a cricket fight with exciting fondness,

A candlelight was flickering on the window, and the fenced courtyard outside was shrouded in pitch darkness.

147

病　牛

宋　李纲

耕犁千亩实千箱，

力尽筋疲谁复伤？

但得众生皆得饱，

不辞羸病卧残阳。

A Sick Buffalo

He plowed a thousand acres and the yields filled up a hundred

granaries,

Exhaustion caught up with him yet on his behalf were enlisted

anything but our sympathies.

To relieve men from food scarcities,

He toiled and moiled only to end up lying in the setting sun,

afflicted by wounds and maladies.

钓　台

宋　李清照

巨舰只缘因利往，

扁舟亦是为名来。

往来有愧先生德，

特地通宵过钓台。

Yan Guang, a Man of Integrity

Great ships were cruising for nothing but wealth and fame,

Small boats all for the same.

The virtues of Yan Guang were such as to put everyone to shame,

So they preferred to sail past his memorial temple when totally

dark it had became.

三衢道中

宋 曾几

梅子黄时日日晴，

小溪泛尽却山行。

绿阴不减来时路，

添得黄鹂四五声。

On My Way to Quzhou

Ripening plums turned yellowish when a long sunny spell was holding sway,

Aboard a boat, I sailed along a stream to its end, where I started forging uphill without delay.

Trees arching over the mountain path were as green and shady as those along the waterway,

But here, sporadic singing came from an exuberance of foliage where orioles had a stay.

墨 梅

宋 张嵲

山边幽谷水边村，

曾被疏花断客魂。

犹恨东风无意思，

更吹烟雨暗黄昏。

Plum Blossoms against a Dark Background

In every waterside village and tranquil valley,

The sight of sparse plum blossoms added to a passer's melancholy.

The east wind was the least helpful especially,

It fueled up the rain, and in it everything looked dim and dusky.

池州翠微亭

宋 岳飞

经年尘土满征衣，

特特寻芳上翠微。

好水好山看不足，

马蹄催趁月明归。

Cuiwei Pavilion at Chizhou

After years of battling, perpetually clinging to my cloak was a
layer of dust,

Astride on a horse, I went on a tour of Cuiwei Pavilion, putting
aside every other must.

The landscape was so beautiful that on me a magic spell it cast,

The clip—clop of my horse a reminder, I had to tear myself away
and the moon witnessed my return to the barracks at last.

题 临 安 邸

宋　林升

山外青山楼外楼，

西湖歌舞几时休？

暖风熏得游人醉，

直把杭州作汴州。

A Poem Inscribed on the Wall
of an Inn in Hangzhou

Beyond eyeshot extend undulating mountains, as well as the
pavilions and terraces,

Beside the West Lake, fiddling and feasting seem everlasting with
entertainers vying to show their paces.

Intoxicated in the soft breeze, the dignitaries are going on the
batter and making short graces,

Their concern is nothing about recovering Bianzhou, the fallen
Capital, but clinging to Hangzhou, a last delusive oasis.

示 儿

宋 陆游

死去元知万事空，

但悲不见九州同。

王师北定中原日，

家祭无忘告乃翁。

A Last Wish

I know anything posthumous means nothing for the dead,

The fact that our country is still split and occupied makes me sad.

Should one day our army recover the lost territory and expel the

northern nomad,

On my sacrificial day, do inform me of this news so glad.

十一月四日风雨大作

宋 陆游

僵卧孤村不自哀，

尚思为国戍轮台。

夜阑卧听风吹雨，

铁马冰河入梦来。

A Poem Composed on a Stormy Day

In a remote village, I was lying stiffly in bed, feeling anything but self−pity,

For my mind was set exclusively on doing my part in defending my country.

With the sound of wind and rain vibrating in my ears, I lay disturbed emotionally,

Dozing off, I dreamed of crossing a frozen river on my armored horse to charge the enemy.

冬夜读书示子聿

宋　陆游

古人学问无遗力，

少壮工夫老始成。

纸上得来终觉浅，

绝知此事要躬行。

Thoughts Shared with My Son
after a Winter–night's Reading

A scholar in the past never got slackened in his study,

The achievement to the credit of an old proved the fruit of his

lifelong assiduity.

Knowledge acquired from books was not everything actually,

To perceive this world, one had to test it in the reality.

读　书

宋　陆游

归志宁无五亩园，

读书本意在元元。

灯前目力虽非昔，

犹课蝇头二万言。

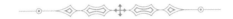

Reading

I aspire for anything but a peaceful retirement on a small farm in
the country,

I've been reading hard for the sake of those in the depth of misery.

Though my eyesight much poorer than yesterday,

Still I've seen through the reading task of twenty thousand
characters, each barely the size of a fly's body.

剑门道中遇微雨

宋　陆游

衣上征尘杂酒痕，

远游无处不消魂。

此身合是诗人未？

细雨骑驴入剑门。

In a Drizzle on My Way to Jianmen Pass

A long trek had bestrewed a layer of dust on my wine–stained garment,

Every place I set foot on presented a look of bewailment.

Did it mean I would end up helpless but to compose poems as a vent?

Astride on a donkey, I kept advancing in a drizzle to the Jianmen Pass and through it I went.

梅花绝句·其一

宋 陆游

闻道梅花坼晓风，

雪堆遍满四山中。

何方可化身千亿，

一树梅花一放翁。

The First *Plum Blossoms*

I hear that a morning breeze has awakened plums into blossom full
and showy,

Snow whiteness is sprawling over all mountains in the country.

Should there be a spell turning me from one into quite a many,

Each before one tree in admiration of its purity.

梅花绝句·其二

宋　陆游

幽谷那堪更北枝，

年年自分着花迟。

高标逸韵君知否，

正是层冰积雪时。

The Second *Plum Blossoms*

A plum tree with a bough stretching north most is standing at a

shady corner of a hidden valley,

Each year this branch blooms late regardlessly.

So aloof are its grace and dignity,

Its flowers start unfolding in defiance of a world snowy and icy.

秋夜将晓出篱门迎凉有感二首·其一

宋　陆游

迢迢天汉西南落，

喔喔邻鸡一再鸣。

壮志病来消欲尽，

出门搔首怆平生。

The First *A Deplorer in Autumn Coolness Before Dawn*

In the southwest is setting the Milky Way spreading seemingly to
infinity,

A rooster next door keeps crowing repeatedly.

Illness has depleted my ambition of recovering the occupied
territory,

Scratching my head in the open, I cannot but sigh over the fact that
my lifelong struggle is a mere futility.

秋夜将晓出篱门迎凉有感二首·其二

宋　陆游

三万里河东入海，

五千仞岳上摩天。

遗民泪尽胡尘里，

南望王师又一年。

The Second *A Deplorer in Autumn Coolness Before Dawn*

The Yellow River is rolling eastward into the sea across the vast expanse of the continent,

Mountains of dizzy height are rising to scrape the firmament.

People in the north are groaning and gasping under the reign of a Tartar tyrant,

Scarcely a year passes when they don't turn southward for their king's army, despite their pray in vain for the coming of that moment.

四时田园杂兴·其一

宋　范成大

昼出耘田夜绩麻，

村庄儿女各当家。

童孙未解供耕织，

也傍桑阴学种瓜。

The First *Rural Life in Early Summer*

Everyday weeding the field and every night making hemp rope,

With their respective task, all villagers, men and women, have to

cope.

For a child, farming and weaving are still beyond his scope,

Under a shady mulberry tree, a way to grow melons he's trying to

grope.

四时田园杂兴·其二

宋 范成大

梅子金黄杏子肥，

麦花雪白菜花稀。

日长篱落无人过，

惟有蜻蜓蛱蝶飞。

The Second *Rural Life in Early Summer*

Trees are heavy with fruits, plums turning golden and apricots fleshy,

Buckwheat blossoms look a sea of whiteness while rape flowers pale in density.

The rising of the sun is contracting the shade of fences, and by them passes nobody,

Yet over them butterflies and dragonflies are dancing with intimacy.

小　池

宋　杨万里

泉眼无声惜细流，

树阴照水爱晴柔。

小荷才露尖尖角，

早有蜻蜓立上头。

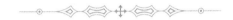

A Little Fountain

Out from the mouth of a spring, water is flowing slowly and quietly,

as if begrudging its resources,

Trees overshadow the fountain, greeting this lovely day with many

graces.

Straining to bloom are the burgeoning lotuses,

On them have landed dragonflies gravitating to their fragrances.

舟过安仁

宋　杨万里

一叶渔船两小童，

收篙停棹坐船中。

怪生无雨都张伞，

不是遮头是使风。

Sailing Past Anren

Two lads were seen in a small fishing vessel,

Putting aside oars and pole, they sat leisurely in the middle.

Umbrellas opened in a rainless day seemed such a puzzle,

To think twice, they meant nothing about keeping off the rain but

to sail before the wind, a truth so simple.

晓出净慈寺送林子方·其一

宋　杨万里

出得西湖月尚残，

荷花荡里柳行间。

红香世界清凉国，

行了南山却北山。

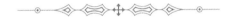

The First *A Morning Send-off of Lin Zifang at Jingci Temple*

As we strolled off the West Lake, a waning moon was still in the
sky,

Weaving our way through lotus ponds, we roamed a path with
willows flanking by.

In a flower realm where fragrance and coolness would never die,

Going downhill here, uphill there we climbed high.

晓出净慈寺送林子方·其二

宋　杨万里

毕竟西湖六月中，

风光不与四时同。

接天莲叶无穷碧，

映日荷花别样红。

The Second *A Morning Send-off of Lin Zifang at Jingci Temple*

Everyone agrees that in June, the West Lake is the most fascinating place,

Distinguished from those of other months is its scene with the most bewitching grace.

Extending beyond horizon are the green lotus leaves huddling the water surface,

The flowers bathed in sunlight seem many a red face.

春 日

宋 朱熹

胜日寻芳泗水滨，

无边光景一时新。

等闲识得东风面，

万紫千红总是春。

A Spring Day

A fine day I roamed a riverside, admiring the beauty of a spring day,

The enchanting landscape took on a fresh look, stretching endlessly far away.

Finally came a time when east wind held sway,

Flowers in full bloom turned a sea of colors glowing in full play.

活水亭观书有感二首·其一

宋　朱熹

半亩方塘一鉴开，

天光云影共徘徊。

问渠哪得清如许？

为有源头活水来。

The First *Reading Under a Pavilion*

Like in a mirror, everything is clearly seen in a small square–
shaped pond,

It ripples gently, and reflections of the sun and clouds twist to
respond.

Transparent to the bottom is the water, and of it I'm so fond,

Why so limpid? Running water finds its way here from far beyond.

活水亭观书有感二首·其二

宋 朱熹

昨夜江边春水生，

艨艟巨舰一毛轻。

向来枉费推移力，

此日中流自在行。

The Second *Reading Under a Pavilion*

The river was swollen with spring flood last night,

Compared to its mighty force, a great ship thereon was but a feather light.

Usually it was the most exhausting to tow it off its anchoring site,

But then it was sailing at ease on the river, free from whatever held it tight.

劝 学 诗

宋 朱熹

少年易老学难成，

一寸光阴不可轻。

未觉池塘春草梦，

阶前梧叶已秋声。

In Persistent Pursuit of Studies

Often you will end up unaccomplished in studies while your youth
has flashed by,

Every minute is such a treasure that you must use it before let it
fly.

When the pond is still dreaming that the lushly green spring is
hard to die,

Leaves above my doorsteps are rustling in the wind, foreboding the
advent of autumn on the sly.

172

乡 村 四 月

宋　翁卷

绿遍山原白满川，

子规声里雨如烟。

乡村四月闲人少，

才了蚕桑又插田。

A Rural Scene in April

Against a verdant mountain, paddy fields are bathed in bright sunlight,

The mellowness of cuckoos adds to the appeal of a drizzly pastoral sight.

In April, an idler is the last man you see in the countryside,

Farmers are always busy rearing silkworms and planting rice, everyday till the eventide.

淮村兵后

宋　戴复古

小桃无主自开花，

烟草茫茫带晚鸦。

几处败垣围故井，

向来一一是人家。

A War–torn Village

Against a sight of desolation, a peach tree was blooming regardlessly,

Over a mist–shrouded village running to weeds, crows were hovering threateningly.

Around an abandoned well scattered the ruins of houses, a sight wretched and shabby,

Otherwise snug homes where people were basking in the love of their family.

有 约

宋 赵师秀

黄梅时节家家雨，

青草池塘处处蛙。

有约不来过夜半，

闲敲棋子落灯花。

An Appointment to Keep

Plums turned yellowish when a rainy spell was holding sway everywhere,

Frogs were croaking in the grass thriving around ponds here and there.

Midnight struck yet my friend didn't show up, and that the prior appointment was broken I became aware,

A chess piece I was playing with dropped on the table and the shock brought down a blob of wax off the candle flare.

庆泉庵桃花

宋　谢枋得

寻得桃源好避秦，

桃红又见一年春。

花飞莫遣随流水，

怕有渔郎来问津。

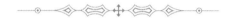

Peach Blossoms at Qingquan Nunnery

This utopia provides us a refuge from the tyranny of the Qin
Empire,

Another spring rolling around, peach trees have burst into blossom
as red as fire.

We dread to see the flowers fall, and their drifting off downstream
is by all odds our last desire,

In that fishermen may track them upstream to where we retire.

蚕 妇 吟

宋 谢枋得

子规啼彻四更时，

起视蚕稠怕叶稀。

不信楼头杨柳月，

玉人歌舞未曾归。

Lamentations of a Silkworm Keeper

At the small hours, the air was reverberating to cuckoos' call,

She got up to feed the silkworms with mulberry leaves lest they might have consumed theirs all.

A bright moon was hanging slightly above trees and buildings tall,

Girls' sweet singing was wafting up from behind a rich family's wall.

武 夷 山 中

宋　谢枋得

十年无梦得还家，

独立青峰野水涯。

天地寂寥山雨歇，

几生修得到梅花？

A Seclusive Life in Mount Wuyi

For ten years I've severed all ties with this world, not even dreaming of a reunion with my family,

Now I'm standing aloof on the peak of a green mountain overlooking an open water stretching boundlessly.

The rain petering out, peace seems to reign over everything earthly,

To be as noble and unsullied as plum blossoms, I have a long way yet to go, more than one lifetime definitely.

寒 菊

宋 郑思肖

花开不并百花丛，

独立疏篱趣未穷。

宁可枝头抱香死，

何曾吹落北风中。

Chrysanthemums

Blooming in autumn, she distinguishes herself as a peerless flower,

Growth beside a sparse hedge has added to her unrivaled charisma.

She would rather cling to her branch and fade with lingering aroma,

Than yield to the north wind and flake down in dishonor.

绝 句

宋 志南

古木阴中系短篷，

杖藜扶我过桥东。

沾衣欲湿杏花雨，

吹面不寒杨柳风。

A Quatrain

I tied my boat to a tree old and shady,

On a cane, I hobbled across a bridge and then eastward through a

charming spring scenery.

Apricot blossoms were thriving in a soft drizzle moistening my robe

slightly,

Willows were swaying their branches in a balmy breeze caressing

my face cozily.

雪梅·其一

宋 卢梅坡

梅雪争春未肯降，

骚人搁笔费评章。

梅须逊雪三分白，

雪却输梅一段香。

The First *Snow and Plum Blossoms*

In early spring, plum blossoms and snowflakes are vying to
outshine each other,

So evenly matched are they that the poet finds it a headache to
decide the winner.

The latter stands unbeaten in that it's slightly whiter,

The former excels with a scent much sweeter.

雪梅·其二

宋 卢梅坡

有梅无雪不精神，

有雪无诗俗了人。

日暮诗成天又雪，

与梅并作十分春。

The Second *Snow and Plum Blossoms*

Plum blossoms look less lively without the foil of snow,

For that sake, he who cannot write a poem proves a creature with a

taste poor and low.

Finally comes out my composition when snowflakes are drifting

down in the sunset glow,

Complementing each other, they two put on a greatest spring show.

临平泊舟

元　黄庚

客舟系缆柳阴旁，

湖影侵篷夜气凉。

万顷波光摇月碎，

一天风露藕花香。

Dropping Anchor at Linping

A willow was overshadowing an anchored passenger ship,

Gradually seeping into the cabin were water's chill and night's nip.

The lake rolling up and down, the moon's reflection twisted only to rip,

Wind relenting at night, the scent of lotuses wafted up and lingered before my nose tip.

到 京 师

元 杨载

城雪初消荠菜生，

角门深巷少人行。

柳梢听得黄鹂语，

此是春来第一声。

In the Capital

In the Capital, snow is melting and shepherd's purse sprouting,

To the general tumult of the city, the backstreet I live forms a

contrast so striking.

Atop a willow, orioles are singing and chatting,

To usher in the spring, they send the first greeting.

墨 梅

元 王冕

吾家洗砚池头树，

朵朵花开淡墨痕。

不要人夸颜色好，

只留清气满乾坤。

Darkish Plum Blossoms

Beside the ink−rinsing tank of my home stands a plum tree,

In bloom, all the flowers are tinged darkish to a slight degree.

They look such a great color, and to that everyone may agree,

Between heaven and earth, their refreshing fragrance is floating

free.

题龙阳县青草湖

元　唐珙

西风吹老洞庭波，

一夜湘君白发多。

醉后不知天在水，

满船清梦压星河。

A Poem Inscribed to Dongting Lake

Rustling autumn wind has dulled the luster of Dongting Lake,

Likewise, grievance that of Xiangjun, a fairy lady, whose hair has greyed also for that sake.

Tipsy, I see stars twinkling in the water, a vision I can't take,

Sleepiness coming over me, I dream of couching on the Galaxy till the moment I wake.

石 灰 吟

明 于谦

千锤万凿出深山，
烈火焚烧若等闲。
粉身碎骨全不怕，
要留清白在人间。

A Eulogy of Lime

Quarried from the depth of a mountain, limestones have stood
severe chiseling and hammering,
As a frequent occurrence, they're subject to flames for refining and
tempering.
They dread to face anything but smashing and grinding,
Like the white lime, I disdain anything begriming and corrupting.

题　画

明　沈周

碧水丹山映杖藜，

夕阳犹在小桥西。

微吟不道惊溪鸟，

飞入乱云深处啼。

A Poem Inscribed on a Painting

Shambling along a mountain path on a cane, I was feasting my eyes on clear waters and fall colors,

Setting to the west of a small bridge, the sun was relenting in dying embers.

Unexpectedly, my humming startled aquatic birds of different features,

They fled screaming skyward into clouds of irregular figures.

拜 年

明　文征明

不求见面惟通谒，

名纸朝来满敝庐。

我亦随人投数纸，

世情嫌简不嫌虚。

New Year's Regards

We deliver cards to hold each other in regard instead of coming in
person to that end,

As a result, everywhere in my house are littering delicate ones sent
or to send.

Like it or lump it, I cannot but follow this trend,

In this world, usually it is to these useless formalities that we have
to attend.

189

言 志

明 唐寅

不炼金丹不坐禅，

不为商贾不耕田。

闲来写就青山卖，

不使人间造孽钱。

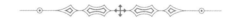

My Aspiration

I don't pursue Buddhist enlightenment, neither do I practice alchemy,

I don't go into business, neither do I engage in husbandry.

If necessary, I sell what I paint for bread daily,

By no means shall I do anything in exchange for dirty money.

画 鸡

明　唐寅

头上红冠不用裁，

满身雪白走将来。

平生不敢轻言语，

一叫千门万户开。

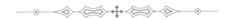

A Rooster

To buck him up, his red comb beats a tailor-made hat,

He struts about, white-clad.

Seldom does he crow for this reason or that,

Once he does, all households will fling their doors open in no time

flat.

菊 花

明 唐寅

故园三径吐幽丛，

一夜玄霜坠碧空。

多少天涯未归客，

尽借篱落看秋风。

Chrysanthemums

Overnight burst into blossom the chrysanthemums arching over the
three trails of my garden,

In defiance of a bitter frost falling all of a sudden.

For those wandering a foreign land loneliness−laden,

Quite impressive were the flowers surviving the cold autumn wind
holding sway under heaven.

美 人 对 月

明　唐寅

斜髻娇娥夜卧迟，

梨花风静鸟栖枝。

难将心事和人说，

说与青天明月知。

A Beauty under the Moon

Her hair in a loose bun, a fair maid was staying up late,

A pear tree and a bird thereon were quieting down in the wind to abate.

For want of perceptive ears, she was saddled with bitterness to accumulate,

So she bared her heart to the bright moon in the clear sky by way of a struggle against her fate.

题《墨葡萄图》

明　徐渭

半生落魄已成翁，

独立书斋啸晚风。

笔底明珠无处卖，

闲抛闲掷野藤中。

A Poem Inscribed on the Painting *Purple Grapes*

A despondent greybeard, I had run half my race floundering,
One night, I stood alone in my study while the wind was howling.
Both castaways were my sparkling compositions and the pearl–like grapes in the painting,
One ended up in a trash bin shredding and the other in a vineyard rotting.

马 上 作

明　戚继光

南北驱驰报主情，

江花边草笑平生。

一年三百六十日，

多是横戈马上行。

My Army Life, a Poem Composed on Horseback

To live up to the expectations of His Majesty, I've ridden through
many a land and fought in many a battle,
Both bright—colored riversides and weed—infested frontiers have
witnessed a warrior on his mettle.
For most time of year every single,
Weapon in hand, I've been rolling on in the saddle.

让 墙 诗

清 张英

千里捎书只为墙，

让他三尺又何妨。

长城万里今犹在，

不见当年秦始皇。

Comity

Far away comes a family letter about a neighborhood border tiff,

To solve that, a little concession on our part is not a big if.

The age-old Great Wall, a frontier defense, remains standing stiff,

The Emperor decreeing the above project have long passed away,

his Empire falling at a whiff.

竹 石

清　郑燮

咬定青山不放松，
立根原在破岩中。
千磨万击还坚劲，
任尔东西南北风。

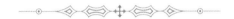

Tough Bamboos

Striking deep into the mountain, bamboos stand firm and upright,

Despite the rocky soil, they take root in space tight.

Exposed to the elements, bamboos put up an unyielding fight,

Summer blowing or winter howling, they fortify against it with a heart light.

墨竹图题诗

清 郑燮

衙斋卧听萧萧竹，

疑是民间疾苦声。

些小吾曹州县吏，

一枝一叶总关情。

A Poem Inscribed on the Painting *Ink-sketched Bamboos*

Resting in my office, I heard bamboo leaves rustling in the breeze,

A sound reminding me that the helpless disadvantaged were

whimpering for want of subsistence needs.

For minor officials as many as grass seeds,

The humble people's concerns were always important deeds.

论　诗

清　赵翼

李杜诗篇万口传，

至今已觉不新鲜。

江山代有才人出，

各领风骚数百年。

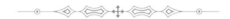

On Poetry

The poems of Li Bai and Du Fu have been on the lips of everybody,

They're so widely read that we find in them anything but novelty.

This world has never run short of geniuses in their respective territory,

Where his or her achievements have been resonating for more than one century.

村 居

清 高鼎

草长莺飞二月天，

拂堤杨柳醉春烟。

儿童散学归来早，

忙趁东风放纸鸢。

A Rural Picture

Grass shooting out and birds flying about herald the advent of February,

Willow twigs drooping over the riverbank, I'm intoxicated in the bewitching spring scenery.

Children are dismissed from school early, so going home not a worry,

Rejoicing at the east wind rising, they disperse to fly kites, all in a hurry.